a photographic
journey through

WOLFEBORO
the Oldest Summer Resort in America

WOLFEBORO
the Oldest Summer
Resort in America

published by Wolfeboro Gifts, an imprint of Red Bicycle Publications

Copyright © 2021 Wolfeboro Gifts

All rights reserved. No part of this book may be reproduced in any form or by any electronic or mechanical means, including information storage and retrieval systems, without permission in writing from the publisher.

ISBN 978-1-7376407-1-4

Library of Congress Control Number 2021920783

Printed in Grand Rapids, Michigan, the United States of America.
First printing 2021

Published by:
  Wolfeboro Gifts
  P.O. Box 30380
  Alexandria, VA 22310-8380

Visit us at www.wolfeborogifts.com

Wolfeboro Gifts is an imprint of Red Bicycle Publications. Learn more about our suite of publications and genres at www.redbicyclepublications.com

WOLFEBORO
the Oldest Summer Resort in America

What is your memory of Wolfeboro?

Hot dogs at dockside. Ice cream cones anywhere.

Perhaps it's skiing, water or snow. Golfing. Baseball, softball, pickleball, or tennis. Hockey, field or ice.

Or picnicking with a view of the lake. Boating in the sunshine. Camping. Smelling wood smoke and eating s'mores.

Maybe it's growing up. Raising a family. Running a business, local or national. Retiring.

It could also be parades, patriotism, civic pride, and community engagement. Thoughts of a big small town.

I found my way to Wolfeboro in 2003 when I came to meet my husband's family before we were married. Lucky for me not only did I fall in love with my husband, but also with a family and a town. After taking a photography course in high school and working in a camera store as my first paying job, I've been taking pictures ever since. I always travel with my camera. Coming to Wolfeboro was no different. My camera came too.

While Wolfeboro, for me, was about visiting family, photography slowly crept in. I found myself taking longer and longer drives in and around town with my husband. We'd make frequent stops to get out and hike the Cotton Valley Trail or walk around downtown and dockside. Before long, I wasn't just taking pictures. Wolfeboro wasn't just a place. I started to see the character and personality present in Wolfeboro's landmarks. Icons like the town hall, Carpenter School, and the train station were just as alive and central to the town as the people. If I were writing a story, these iconic sites would be the central characters. Since I'm taking pictures, these iconic structures are visual anchors. You can't think of Wolfeboro without them.

Just like dressing in layers comes in handy for New England weather, I think of photographs in layers too. While iconic landmarks are the base layer, next come the moods and energy of a scene. I look for how the sunlight or clouds, for example, might create a restful or more dynamic feeling in an image. Weather and the seasons always add to the mood. I love how you can visit Cate Park in the summer and there's an energy with sunny, bright skies, flowers blooming, children running, and picnic tables humming with vacation-feeling conversations. Cate Park in the autumn has a completely different mood. The Park is dressed in golden hues yet presents as shy and still in the drizzly rain.

Finally are the added layers of details. Wolfeboro is far more than the picture postcard shot. Wolfeboro is also well accessorized! You can't appreciate Wolfeboro fully without noting the flags on Main Street and the memorials around town that connect past to present. It's the welcome signs on the street, wreaths on the doors, and reflections in the windows. What makes Wolfeboro feel like Wolfeboro is hearing pianos and sea gulls. It's also catching the briefest savory whiff of fresh baked goods or sweet ice cream as you walk downtown. Of course, Wolfeboro isn't

Wolfeboro without the people — whether they welcome you by name or appreciate your presence in anonymity. As my husband and I continued our drives in and around town over the years, I enjoyed finding the details and seeing how Wolfeboro changes her accessories with the seasons.

Now that I've shared some of my history and photographic appreciation of Wolfeboro, here's some history about the town:

The Town of Wolfeboro was granted on October 5, 1759, settled in 1768, and incorporated in 1770. The town was named (originally Wolfeborough) in honor of General James Wolfe who had been victorious (but killed) at the Battle of the Plains of Abraham in 1759 during the French and Indian War. Colonial Governor John Wentworth, his nephew, established an estate on the site, known as Kingswood. Built in 1771 beside what is now called Lake Wentworth, this was the first summer country estate in northern New England and is the reason Wolfeboro calls itself "The Oldest Summer Resort in America."

In the more than 260 years since its founding, Wolfeboro has become a popular seasonal destination for people from around the world. Heads of state and famous actors routinely join those seeking escape from urban locations for a few days or weeks or months (or years) on the shores of Lake Winnipesaukee, the largest lake in the State of New Hampshire.

Lake Winnipesaukee is an integral part of Wolfeboro's livelihood. The Abenaki name Winnipesaukee (often spelled Winnipiseogee in earlier centuries) means either "smile of the Great Spirit" or "beautiful water in a high place." Both translations perfectly capture the spirit and vitality of the lake and its more than 250 islands. Wolfeboro Bay creates a small northerly bulge in the shoreline of the eastern edge of Winnipesaukee. A series of smaller lakes and streams connects Wolfeboro Bay to Lake Wentworth, Wolfeboro's second-largest body of water at more than 3,000 acres.

Wolfeboro began as a farming community in what is now the North Wolfeboro area known as Dimon's Corner, a settlement on the stage route from Dover to Conway. Lumber and the growth and sales of apple products were a large part of early industry. To the south, Wolfeboro Falls became known as "Slab City" for its wood-related manufacturing, a major local industry until the early 20th century.

Although most now consider the bridge downtown that separates North and South Main Streets as the center of Wolfeboro activity, early Wolfeboro boasted several distinct neighborhoods and activity centers in and around Dimon's Corner, Goose Corner, South Wolfeboro, Pleasant Valley, Wolfeboro Falls, and Wolfeboro Center.

As the years passed, lumber processing gave way to the manufacture of textiles, shoes, clay pipes, dairy products, and pewter. The end of the Civil War and the building of the Wolfeboro Railroad in 1872 brought more tourists to Wolfeboro, and the industry began to flourish. Wolfeboro's first major hotel, The Pavilion, was built in 1850 and was followed by several others. Just over 20 years later in 1872, the Mt. Washington began to ply the waters of Lake Winnipesaukee transporting residents and visitors across The Big Lake.

In 1790, Wolfeboro had just 447 residents. Today, Wolfeboro is the year-round home for over 6,400 with tens of thousands more seasonal residents and visitors.

Now that you know a bit more about Wolfeboro, let's step out the door and take a drive in and around town. We'll begin on Main Street and travel rural roads too. As the Wolfeboro sign welcomes you, let your preoccupations fade away. Relax. Take a deep breath of fresh air. Let's go!

-LS

downtown

"For any American who had the great and priceless privilege of being raised in a small town there always remains with him nostalgic memories."

- Dwight D. Eisenhower

Wolfeboro's downtown welcomes you with a quaint, historic Main Street with storefronts that smile and flags that wave. If downtown Wolfeboro had a color palette it would include primary hues of lakeside blues, sunshine yellow, woodsy brown, and dusty autumn red. In the summer, there's an energy to Main Street. Visitors stroll by reflective windows and planter boxes with vibrant flowers and American flags. Faint chords of piano music and the scent of baked goods and freshly scooped ice cream fill the air. Main Street is the perfect place for a leisurely stroll and diversions of the pocketbook.

Wolfeboro's town hall and municipal office building is formally known as the Brewster Memorial Hall, hearkening to its ownership by the Brewster Trust. In addition to the town offices, this building has also housed the Wolfeboro District Court, the Wolfeboro Public Library, private businesses, and a 385-seat movie theater since its construction in 1890.

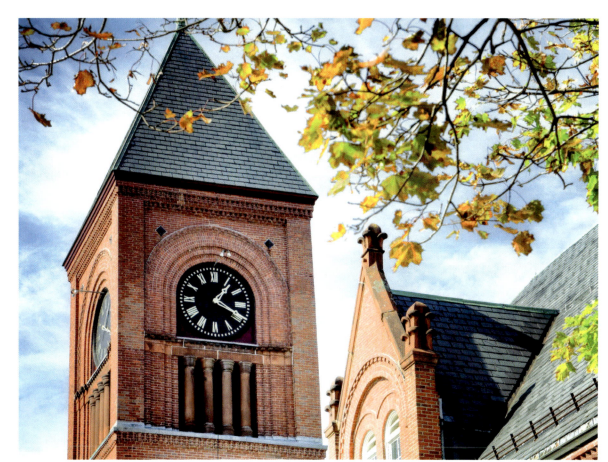
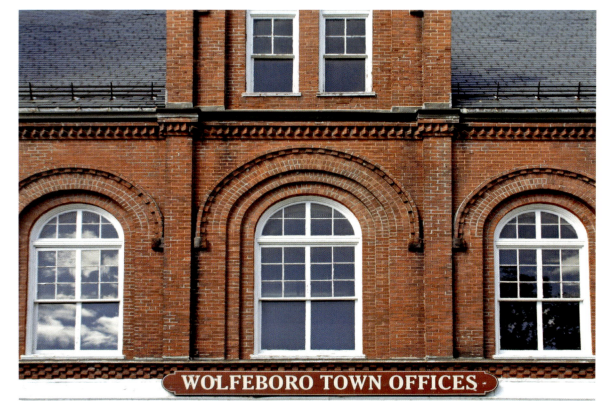

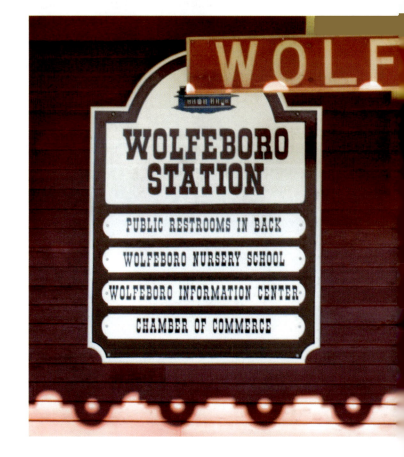

This iconic Victorian-era railroad station was constructed in 1872.
It was initially built to support the Eastern Railroad (which later became the Boston & Maine Railroad). As rail services diminished and later ended, the building has been occupied by the Wolfeboro Chamber of Commerce, commercial businesses, the Wolfeboro Railroad Club, and a nursery school and youth center.

Molly the Trolley carries passengers on a 45-minute narrated tour of Wolfeboro featuring views of Lake Winnipesaukee. Molly stops at many of Wolfeboro's museums and points of interest, dockside, and downtown.

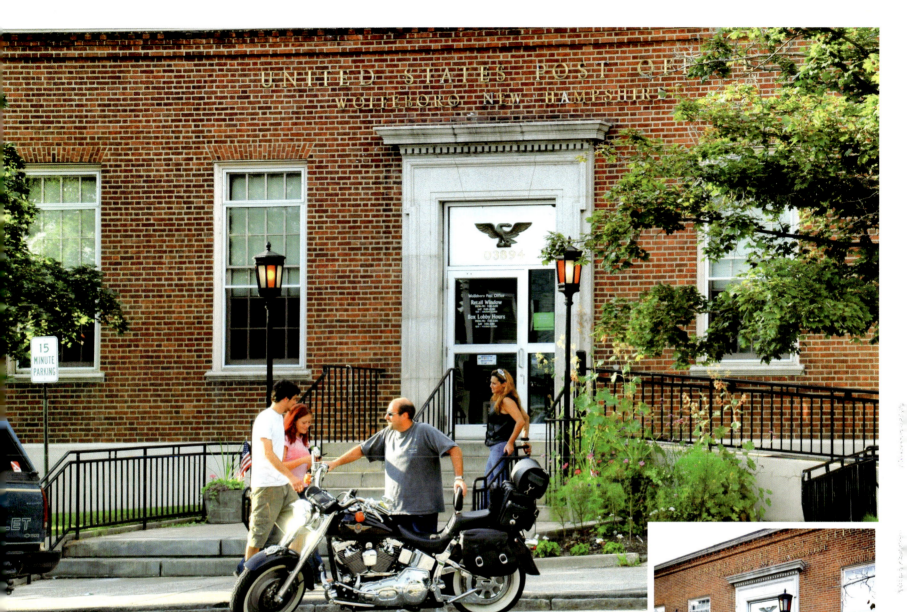

HENRY MORGENTHAU JR
SECRETARY OF THE TREASURY

JAMES A FARLEY
POSTMASTER GENERAL

LOUIS A SIMON
SUPERVISING ARCHITECT

NEAL A MELICK
SUPERVISING ENGINEER

1936

The Wolfeboro Post Office building, a landmark to Wolfeboro residents and visitors alike, has been the town's Post Office since 1936. Before that the Wolfeboro Post Office was located across the street in what is now known as the Avery Building.

downtown | 13

"Childhood is the small town everyone came from."

- Garrison Keillor

South Main Street's architecture
reminds you that you are in a historic New England village.

Hunter's IGA (now Shop 'n Save)

was founded in 1979 as the quintessential small-town grocery. Over the years, it has become Wolfeboro's most well-known grocery store due in part to its proximity to the Wolfeboro town docks. Island-dwellers and boaters can be seen transporting bags of food and beverages from Hunter's to dockside daily.

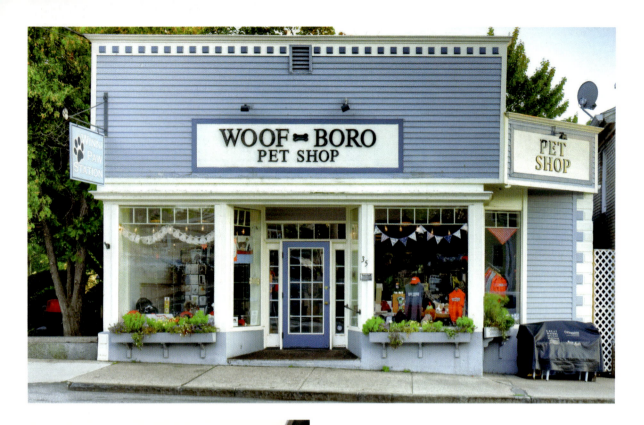

16 | downtown

Bradley's Hardware, Railroad Avenue's "anchor store," is Wolfeboro's longest-running hardware and home repair store.

Blue hues abound downtown, reflecting both Wolfeboro's proximity to water and the water's profound importance to the town and its people.

The Yum Yum Shop has been a Wolfeboro institution since 1948
when "Grandma" Lotte Kelly opened her bake shop. This fixture on North Main Street now scratch bakes specialty doughnuts, bread, pies, cakes, and their famous gingerbread cookies daily. And of course, because this is Wolfeboro, you can get an ice cream to enjoy on their patio or to go.

The Yum Yum Shop's patio also features a hand-carved wooden bench honoring their famous gingerbread cookies.

downtown | 19

The Avery Building

is a Wolfeboro icon between dockside and South Main Street. This three-story building is named after J. Clifton Avery, the founder of a multi-generational insurance agency. The Avery Building has, over time, housed the Wolfeboro Post Office, stores, and residences.

Yellows, browns, flags, and a moose

complete the colonial New England themes you see throughout Wolfeboro.

downtown | 21

It's hard not to feel welcome in Wolfeboro, whether you are a year-round resident, part-time resident, or visitor.

downtown | 23

Perhaps the best-known store in Wolfeboro, Black's Paper Store (or The Paper Store, as it was originally called in the 1940s) sits in a prime location on South Main Street in downtown Wolfeboro. Its colorful awnings beckon shoppers in the summer and provide the backdrop for Wolfeboro's town Christmas tree each winter.

What New England town doesn't have a diner or an inn?
Wolfeboro has long had a typical small-town, family-run diner at the downtown bridge that joins North and South Main Streets. While the names have changed over the years, the family feeling remains.

The Wolfeboro Inn on North Main Street has been providing lodging under several names since the 1930s. It has been featured in national and international publications and is the only property in Wolfeboro to receive a AAA 4-diamond rating. The adjacent Wolfe's Tavern is a go-to watering hole for locals and tourists alike.

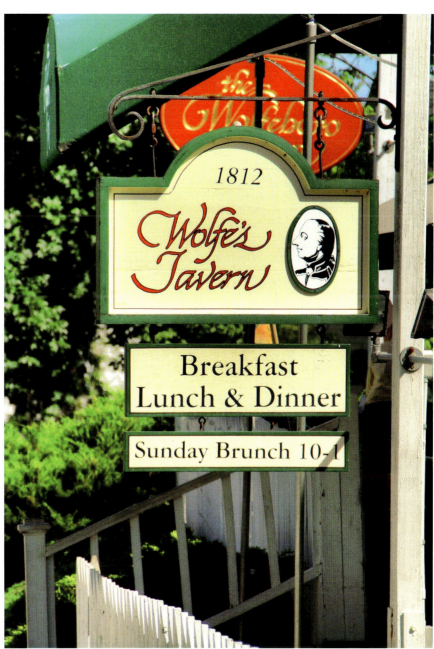

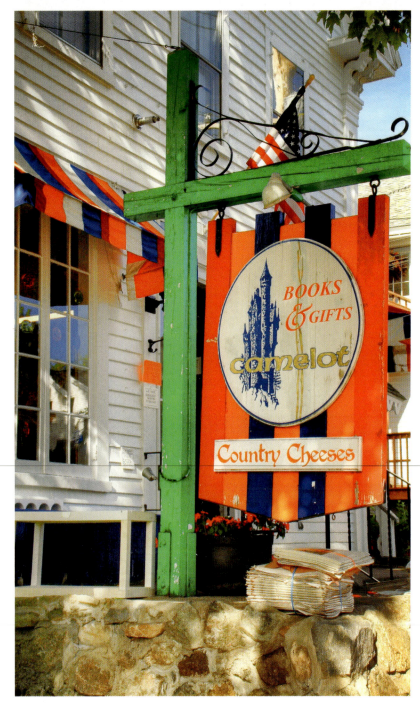

The Camelot Book and Gift Shop was a fixture on North Main Street for many years. In addition to a large selection of books, shoppers could find games, gifts, recordings, and gourmet wine and cheese, with the morning's papers lovingly displayed outside the front window. Established in 1964, Camelot closed its doors in 2008 and for many years was known for the large nutcracker standing guard outside.

Practically across the street, Durgin Stables now houses downtown Wolfeboro's largest bookstore and many other retail stores and offices.

The Country Bookseller, a locally-owned and operated independent bookstore, has a wide variety of fiction and non-fiction titles along with snack and drink offerings. The bookstore often features local authors and hosts book signings and authors' nights throughout the year.

The reflections in the windows of Wolfeboro add to the charm of a walk through downtown. Nearly everywhere you turn, you can see the Town Hall, the Post Office, the Railroad Station, or other Wolfeboro icons - either in front of you or reflected in store windows.

"Save the Wolfeboro Pianos," a project initiated by a local resident and sponsored by the Great Waters Music Festival, has placed pianos throughout Wolfeboro in recent years.

36 | downtown

Bailey's Bubble is known for its ice cream and lines that stretch down Railroad Avenue all summer long. "The Bubble" has been providing a respite from the summer heat since 1994.

dockside

"It is life, I think, to watch the water. A person can learn so many things."

- Nicholas Sparks

Dockside offers space to watch and enjoy Lake Winnipesaukee. Find your spot to sit at the restaurant or with a view from above. You may also choose to get a hot dog, ice cream, or fresh lemonade to go and sit at one of the benches along the docks. In summer, the comings and goings of boats and people watching add to the contemplative pleasure. If arriving in Wolfeboro by the Mount Washington, Dockside is your welcome mat.

Known to locals as "The Mount," every summer the Motor Ship (M/S) Mount Washington connects tourists and residents with stops at the Wolfeboro Town Docks, Alton Bay, Center Harbor, Meredith, and Weirs Beach (Laconia).

dockside | 41

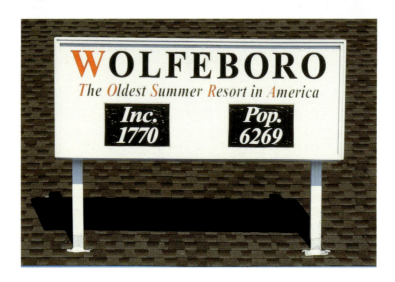

The Wolfeboro sign at dockside
is regularly updated to reflect Wolfeboro's year-round population. Wolfeboro's population increased approximately 200 people between 2010 and 2020.

The higher you go, the better the view. The Wolfeboro Town Docks, known to locals as "dockside," are a series of public docks. There is also a boat launch, parking lot, and easy access to Cate Park and downtown restaurants and retailers. The Mount Washington, Blue Ghost, and other public and private vessels launch from dockside.

Hot Dog Bob
or one of his several predecessors have sold hot dogs, cold drinks, and various other snacks at the Wolfeboro town docks for decades.

"When was the last time you spent a quiet moment just doing nothing — just sitting and looking at the sea, or watching the wind blowing the tree limbs, or waves rippling on a pond, a flickering candle or children playing in the park?"

– Ralph Marston

The boats of the Wolfeboro Fire Rescue Department have protected the lives and property of those on the lakes and islands for decades. The "H. W. Drury" (top) was in service in the 1990s. Its successor (bottom) continues to serve into the 2020s.

"A lake is a landscape's most beautiful and expressive feature. It is Earth's eye; looking into which the beholder measures the depth of his own nature."

- Henry David Thoreau

Dockside at sunset brings magical views of Wolfeboro Bay
and during the summer you will find diners, boaters, shoppers, and everyone else
pausing to take in the beauty of the eastern shore of Lake Winnipesaukee.

cate park

"Parks . . .are the soul of a town."

– Marty Rubin

Cate Park dresses for the seasons. She wears floral skirts in the summer and golden gowns in the fall. In winter, she is covered in snow white, billowy drifts with evergreen trim. She dances at summer concerts. She offers respite for a picnic or a quiet moment to reflect in the fall. At Christmas, she sparkles with glitter and lights. Red ribbons accent her hair. Cate Park's Hallmark moment awaits.

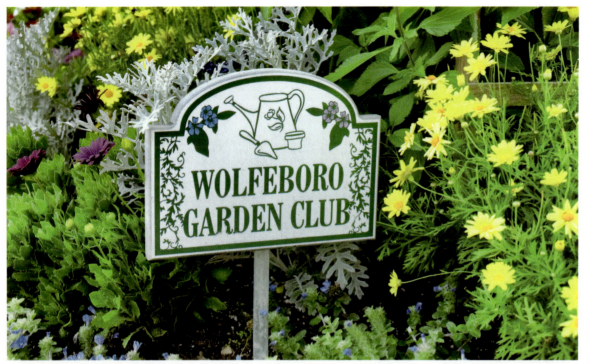

Cate Park was established by the town in 1941 and known as the Lake Front Park. The upper level, formally named the Town Park and closer to South Main Street, is usually also referred to as and/or confused with Cate Park. Together the two parks have been host over the years to numerous fairs, live entertainment, and a small garden tended by local residents.

The Cate Park gazebo, also known as the Community Bandstand, hosts live entertainment in the summer, a perfectly-sized Christmas tree in December, and Hallmark Movie views year-round.

The autumn colors in Cate Park are as spectacular as the autumn colors throughout the rest of Wolfeboro.

Cate Park in the winter
brings peace, serenity, and views of Lake Winnipesaukee as far as the eye can see. If the wind is blowing the right direction, you'll also smell the cozy aroma of wood stoves heating the town's homes.

"Sharing," a bronze sculpture of a grandfather and grandson seated on a bench enjoying an ice cream, feels even more like a Norman Rockwell scene in the mounds of snow.

Pristine snow on a winter's day reminds residents why they have chosen Wolfeboro as their year-round home.

academic Wolfeboro

"Education is simply the soul of a society as it passes from one generation to another."

– G. K. Chesterton

Wolfeboro's educational buildings have hosted generations. Carpenter School, serving the youngest students, gives a nod to Wolfeboro's history. Crescent Lake School welcomes late elementary students with teaching centered on the three "R's" of readiness, respect, and resiliency. Kingswood sets learning in middle, high, and arts buildings. Sprawling athletic fields and the stadium are places that seem to fold past and present together. Finally, Brewster Academy, with buildings that view Lake Winnipesaukee, embraces the beauty of Wolfeboro and shows the important juxtaposition of private and public educational space.

Carpenter School, opened with 10 classrooms in 1925, has educated Wolfeboro's elementary school students for nearly 100 years. By 2021, only students in Grades K-3 attended Carpenter.

The Crescent Lake School
was built when Carpenter School could no longer accommodate all of the district's K-6 grade students. Crescent Lake School had a 2021 Grade 4-6 student population of just over 200.

The Kingswood Regional Middle School, built in 1986-1987 and officially named in 1991, educates students in grades 7 and 8. Until 1986, junior high students attended classes in a portion of the Kingswood High School building.

academic wolfeboro | 77

The Kingswood Regional campus, located on South Main Street, welcomes students in grades 9 through 12 from Wolfeboro, Brookfield, Effingham, Middleton, New Durham, Ossipee, and Tuftonboro. The campus houses the senior high school, the middle high school, an arts center, a vocational school, and athletic fields. Graduating classes have provided gifts including the school's sign and marble benches.

The Kingswood Knights represent southern Carroll County in nearly every competitive sport, including cheerleading, cross country, field hockey, football, golf, soccer, volleyball, skiing, basketball, ice hockey, track, swimming, baseball, softball, lacrosse, tennis, and track and field.

academic wolfeboro | 81

Brewster Academy, founded in 1887, is a private preparatory school offering instruction in grades 9-12. It began as the Wolfeborough and Tuftonborough Academy in 1820. Brewster served as a school for the local population for more than 140 years but transitioned to its current role as an independent school in 1965 when Kingswood Regional High School opened up the street. Today, Brewster attracts students with the promise of being an intellectually diverse and academically challenging community that nurtures curiosity, confidence, collaboration, and character in preparation for lives of meaning and accomplishment.

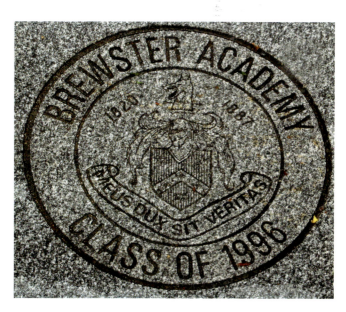

academic wolfeboro | 83

84 | academic wolfeboro

around town

"Living in a rural setting exposes you to so many marvelous things - the natural world and the particular texture of small-town life, and the exhilarating experience of open space."

- Susan Orlean

Exploring Wolfeboro beyond downtown finds museums and historic buildings, picture-postcard, waterside views, and community and civic organizations to appreciate. Wolfeboro simultaneously embraces past and present with memorials, honors to important firsts, and tributes to service. You'll find these landmarks around town and tucked into rural clearings. As you expand your drive around town, you'll discover Wolfeboro's rural character—winding roads, stone walls, roadside stands, bright red doors with wreaths, patriotic displays, and most of all New England spirit.

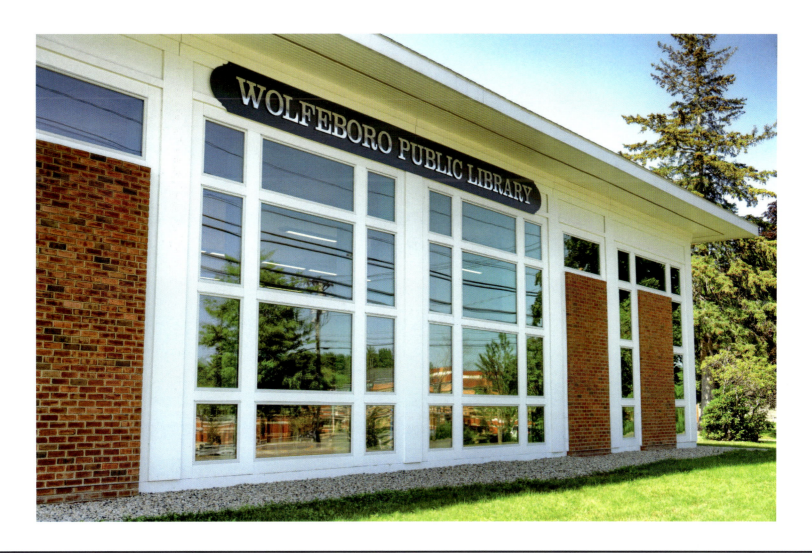

The Clark House Museum, also known as "Clark Park," is a small park that contains the Pleasant Valley Schoolhouse, a fire museum, and the 18th Century Clark House. The buildings are maintained by the Wolfeboro Historical Society and open to visitors during the summer months.

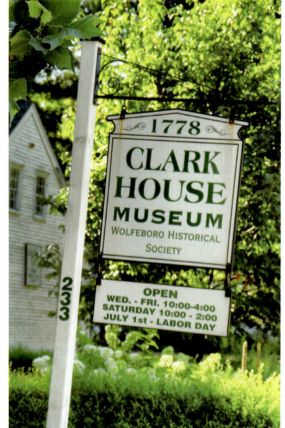
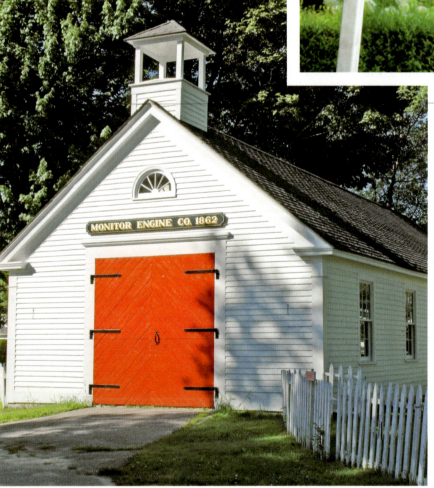

88 | around town

Wolfeboro honors its citizen-soldiers like most New England towns. Located at the intersection of South Main Street and Center Street (also known as Pickering Corner), these memorials pay tribute to soldiers, sailors, airmen, and marines.

Wolfeboro's current heroes,
the members of its Fire Rescue and Police Departments, those who have given the ultimate sacrifice, the medical professionals of Huggins Hospital, and the volunteer citizen first responders who have protected Wolfeboro throughout the years, keep the town and its citizens and guests safe.

90 | around town

Need food?

Morrissey's Front Porch is a family restaurant located on South Main Street in Wolfeboro. Serving traditional New England fare including lobster, fried seafood, turkey dinners, and chowder, they also offer an extensive ice cream selection. This restaurant sits on the site of the former Bailey's Restaurant, a Wolfeboro institution from 1938 until the late 1990s.

Need snacks?

The Corner Store has been selling gas and convenience items at Pickering Corner since 1979. It's a good bet that everyone who has ever been to Wolfeboro in the last 40 years has either gotten gas or stepped foot inside their doors.

around town | 91

Power boats, sailboats, and paddle boats, old and new,
can be found throughout Wolfeboro.

Founded by David M. Wright, the museum that bears his name showcases memorabilia from the 1940s and military artifacts used during wartime. A victory garden sits just outside, boasting that it is "like a share in an airplane factory. It helps with the war and it pays dividends too."

Harriman-Hale
Unit 18 of the American Legion Auxiliary serves Wolfeboro's Veterans from all conflicts.

around town | 93

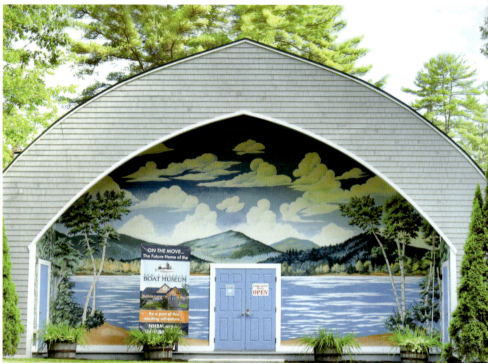

The New Hampshire Boat Museum was founded in 1992 by antique and classic boating enthusiasts who wanted to preserve and share New Hampshire's boating heritage. It found its permanent home in Wolfeboro in 2000 after temporary residence in other Lake Winnipesaukee towns.

The Village Players have produced full-length shows since the 1930s, typically a musical in the fall and other events throughout the year.

Dr. Henry F. Libby founded this nature and history museum in 1912. In addition to its historical collections, the museum contains galleries exhibiting works of New Hampshire artists and hosts regular classes and lectures.

College Road was established in 1771 by Governor John Wentworth, who wanted a highway from his estate in Wolfeborough to Dartmouth College.

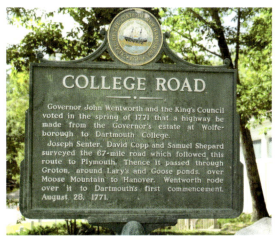

The 12-mile Cotton Valley Rail Trail
begins at the Wolfeboro railroad station (co-located with the Russell C. Chase Bridge Falls Path) and ends at Turntable Park in Wakefield. The most-used portion of the trail runs from downtown Wolfeboro to the Fernald Crossing station and hosts walkers, runners, hikers, cross-country skiers, snowmobilers, and the occasional musher.

Fernald Crossing
marked the location where the Wolfeborough Railroad crossed Route 109 on its way to Brookfield. The station served both as a regular station-stop as well as a flag stop (where the train would stop only upon request).

Red doors abound around Wolfeboro, including these from the Fernald Crossing Railroad Station and the Harriman-Hale American Legion Post 18, and epitomize the colonial and patriotic spirit that permeates Wolfeboro.

The Wolfeboro Centre
Community Church (also known as the Union Meeting House, First Christian Society, and Second Christian Church) was built in 1841 to house the religious activities of a Free Will Baptist and an independent Congregationalist group.

The Cotton Mountain Community Church, built about 1852, also known as the Wolfeborough, Brookfield and Wakefield Meetinghouse, is a historic church on Stoneham Road near the Brookfield town line and a well-preserved example of a rural New England meeting house with vernacular Greek Revival style.

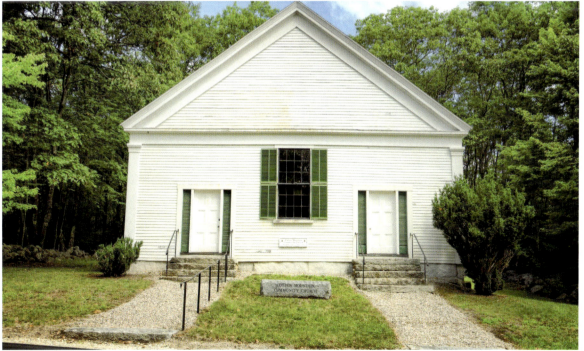

Wolfeboro has been farming for centuries
and today's family farmers keep the tradition alive. You will find everything you need on a drive around town. Spring brings flowers. Berries, corn, and produce follow. Fall brings firewood for the winter. And you can scramble Wolfeboro eggs year-round!

around town | 103

"New Hampshire is one of the birthplaces of American freedom and independence - a place with a love and a passion for liberty."

- Marsha Blackburn

around town | 105

recreation

"Some days are simply made for playing."

- Mary Anne Radmacher

Wolfeboro's doors are always open. No matter the season, recreation opportunities abound. Paddlers of all types dot the lakes and rivers. Jet skis and boats beckon. The thwack and pop of tennis, pickle, and golf balls echo a calling to enthusiasts. Hikers, walkers, and runners can find their place on the Cotton Valley Trail or at the Nick. Lovers of cold, snowy winters certainly aren't left out. There is always an opportunity for snowshoeing and skiing, whether cross country or downhill. So, come outside and play!

Like to paddle?
Wolfeboro has it all.

Canoeing. Kayaking. Paddleboarding. What better way to enjoy the great outdoors while getting exercise and watching the majestic scenery!

You're never too young or too old to appreciate all that Lake Winnipesaukee has to offer. The ways of the Big Lake are passed from generation to generation.

recreation | 111

The bridge in downtown Wolfeboro officially marks the intersection of North and South Main Streets as well as the boundary between "back bay" and "Wolfeboro Bay," otherwise known as Lake Winnipesaukee.

"Fishing the small streams of New Hampshire is a pastime that combines hiking, map reading, and bushwhacking - plenty of it."

- Joseph Monninger

Salmon, rainbow trout, perch and small-mouth bass have all been sighted in and around the waters of Wolfeboro. In just the right spot and just the right time of year, you might also land a bluegill, cusk, crappie, or pickerel.

The Russell C. Chase Bridge Falls Path, constructed in 1990, runs along the old Wolfeborough Railroad bed between the train station and Center Street.

The 12-mile Cotton Valley Rail Trail begins at the Wolfeboro railroad station (co-located with the Russell C. Chase Bridge Falls Path) and ends at Turntable Park in Wakefield. The most-used portion of the trail runs from downtown Wolfeboro to the Fernald Crossing station.

The tennis courts at Foss Field downtown
are the hub of activity not just for Wolfeboro's tennis players. In recent years Wolfeboro has become known for hosting one of the largest pickleball tournaments in the country, with competitors traveling thousands of miles to compete and see all that Wolfeboro and the Lakes Region have to offer.

Prefer wheels?
There is no shortage of places to ride in Wolfeboro. Flat route? Hilly route? Paved? Gravel? Quick ride? Day trip? The Wolfeboro Parks and Recreation Department provides year-round recreation opportunities for residents and visitors of all ages.

Kingswood Golf Club, open to members and the public alike, boasts 18 holes, a practice green, driving range, and an on-site PGA professional.

Every fall you'll also see Kingswood High School's award-winning varsity golf team walking the links.

The Nicholas J. Pernokas Recreational Park ("The Nick") opened in 2007. This 27-acre sports facility includes two baseball diamonds, two softball fields, three multi-use fields, a six-lane running track, a mile-long walking path, two playgrounds, picnic area, dog park, skate park, and a covered pavilion.

The 50-acre Wentworth State Park, one of two state parks in Wolfeboro, is located on Route 109 along the northern shore of Lake Wentworth. It has picnic areas, a public beach, and plentiful parking.

"The blast that swept him came off New Hampshire snow-fields and ice-hung forests. It seemed to have traversed interminable leagues of frozen silence, filling them with the same cold roar and sharpening its edge against the same bitter black-and-white landscape."

- Edith Wharton

Snowfall turns Wolfeboro into a winter sports wonderland for both two- and four-legged residents.

recreation | 121

Winter is about sledding and skiing.
Brewster Academy's hilly terrain makes for fun but safe sledding. The Abenaki Ski Area, located on Route 109A just south of Waumbeck Road, contains a ski slope, hut, outdoor and indoor ice rinks, and the entrance to several cross-country ski trails.

A frozen Lake Winnipesaukee presents many recreational opportunities
including snowmobiling, ice fishing, cross-country skiing, and more.

through the seasons

"Live in each season as it passes; breathe the air, drink the drink, taste the fruit, and resign yourself to the influence of the earth."

- Henry David Thoreau

To really know Wolfeboro, you have to see and experience the seasons. Each season brings a different mood, energy, and story. There are different ways of seeing and being in the summer, fall, and winter. Return to the same spot in the summer sunshine, golden glow of fall, and snowy, gray of winter and you'll see how the dynamics, light, and shades of a place shift. Some say that seasons are underrated. When you really know Wolfeboro, you know differently.

128 | through the seasons

Wolfeboro's Back Bay (left)
is situated between Lake Winnipesaukee and the Smith River. Parts of the original Back Bay were reclaimed and are now a rain garden, town parking lot, athletic fields, and shopping centers.

The Huggins Hospital and Community Aid Street Fair, the quintessential New England local fair, is held annually on the first Friday and Saturday of August. Attendees browse through previously-owned books and collectibles, enjoy mechanical and animal rides, savor foods cooked by their neighbors, and play a round (or seven) of bingo.

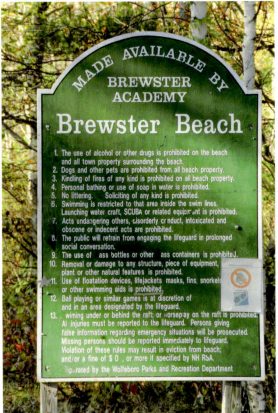

130 | through the seasons

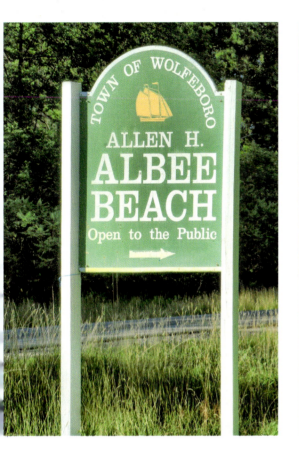

through the seasons | 131

Carry Beach

got its name from the portage of canoes from Winter Harbor to Jockey Cove. Purchased by the town in the late 1950s, this small beach located on Forest Road is beloved by local residents.

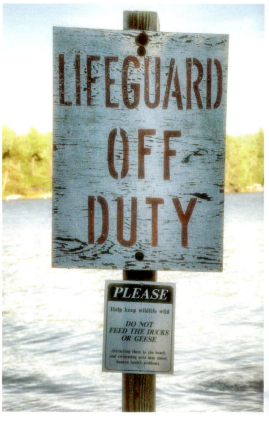

through the seasons | 135

through the seasons | 137

through the seasons | 147

acknowledgments

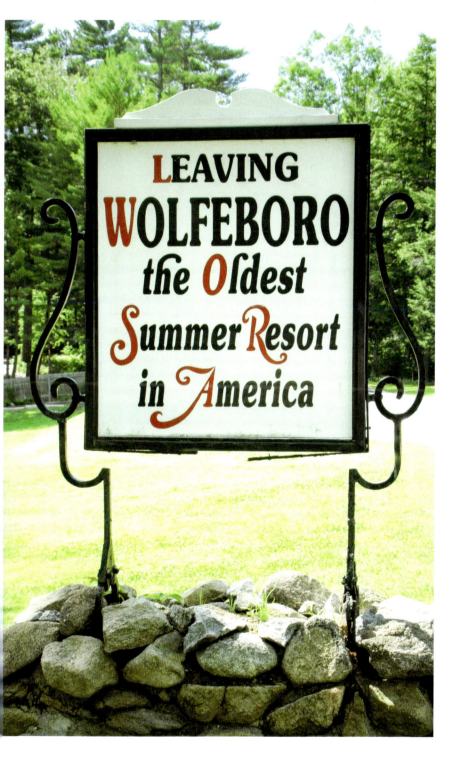

This book would have been impossible without my husband and his family. My husband's extensive knowledge of the town took me to places and roads the typical visitor would never see. The integrated historical references and creative design that links the images into a larger story are fully attributable to him. Wolfeboro is now part of my family. I'm deeply appreciative to Joe and Donna Santoro for their loving welcome and making Wolfeboro feel like it belongs to me now too. Thank you for sharing the beauty of this lakeside town. There are definitely pictures I couldn't have captured without your generous boat trips on Lake Winnipesaukee and your willingness to repeat tours until I could get just the right shot. I'm so incredibly grateful I have you and a place to call home in Wolfeboro.

Lana Santoro is an educator, writer, and photographer. She enjoys traveling and frequent trips to Wolfeboro.